CHINESE
RADICALS

部首

D1292241

PENG'S CHINESE TREASURY

Chinese Radicals

VOLUME 2

concept and cartoons
by
Tan Huay Peng

HEIAN

FIRST AMERICAN EDITION - 1987
Not for sale outside U.S.A.

HEIAN INTERNATIONAL, INC.
P.O. Box 1013
Union City, CA 94587   USA.

First published in Singapore by
Times Books International
Times Centre, 1 New Industrial Road
Singapore 1953

© 1987 **TIMES BOOKS INTERNATIONAL,** Singapore

All rights reserved. No part of this publication
may be reproduced, stored in a retrieval system,
or transmitted, in any form or by any means,
electronic, mechanical, photocopying, recording or
otherwise, without the prior permission of the
publisher.

ISBN 0-89346-292-6

Printed in Singapore.

CHINESE RADICALS

Introduction

Chinese operates differently in many ways from English and other phonetic languages. One of its unique features is that a person having no prior knowledge of Chinese cannot figure out what a Chinese character sounds like from its appearance. With some laboured memory work this initial obstacle may be overcome. Yet an even mightier challenge awaits the learner. Whatever does it mean? A simple yet helpful method of discovering what Chinese characters mean is through studying their radicals.

Chinese dictionaries of old locate characters via stroke count, and by looking under the relevant radical. All Chinese dictionaries have now converted to the Hanyu Pinyin system of reference. Although the function of radicals as dictionary classification is now obsolete, the value of learning about radicals still stands. From a knowledge of them – there exist a total of 214 radicals – a better understanding of those strange composites known as Chinese characters is within reach.

Radicals, or 'root elements', are the foundation of all Chinese characters. They act as common denominators which the mind commits to memory when sizing up the character. Each Chinese character is listed under a particular radical.

米

The 'rice' radical

The 'streaks' radical

雨

The 'rain' radical

皿

The 'vessel' radical

Identifying the radical

Apart from the previous examples, where the radicals are recognised without difficulty, there are others which are not as easy to identify. Which, for instance, is the radical in 歸? As this character is made up of several elements, a few possibilities are present. However, it is found under the 止 radical. Where there are variant forms of radicals, things get even more complicated. The radical in 舒 is 舌, and the radical in 慕 is 心. 舍 and 小 are both variant forms.

Examples

幫　之　事　南　更　舊　將　成　巨　疏　爭　裏

巾　丿　亅　十　曰　臼　寸　戈　工　疋　爪　衣

Position of radicals

Neither does the radical always remain in the same position for each of its character examples. Take these characters, which all share the same radical, 日 , the 'sun' radical.

Characters which function as radicals

About 80 per cent of the radicals also function independently as characters, some examples being:

水　言　山　刀　走　金

水 , water, in its capacity as a radical, gives rise to countless other characters which bear a relationship to water, wetness, and anything liquid.

流　泉　浮　淹　洗　深　淼　港
涕　濕　灣　深　河　江　濱　澡
游泳　　海洋

山 , mountain, produces characters referring to hills and mountains and also to height.

岸 島 峽 峰 峻 岡 崩 岳
峨 巒 峭 巖 嶙 嶺 岔 嶄

Classification

In instances where both elements are radicals, the character would be classified under the radical which determines the meaning.

For the character 悶 , both 門 and 心 are radicals. The 心 radical, from whence emotions and feelings arise, is thus the one under which the character is listed.

Then again, take a character like 酒 . Both 氵 and 酉 are radicals, but 酉 , meaning 'wine', provides the dominant meaning. The character is therefore found under the 'wine' radical.

Clues to meaning

Radicals are not mere decorative elements.
Obviously, in characters which are otherwise purely
phonetic, the radical plays the vital role of
furnishing the meaning.

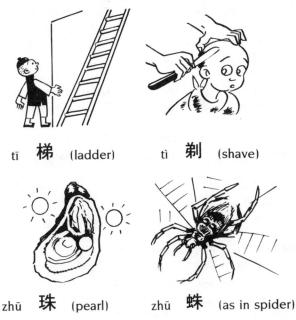

tī 梯 (ladder)   tì 剃 (shave)

zhū 珠 (pearl)   zhū 蛛 (as in spider)

Of course there will be cases where the radical plus
the other element contribute equally to meaning.
The result of combining the 'man' radical with the
character for 'word' creates the character 信, trust or
believe. Similarly, 証 brings together the 'speech'
radical and the character meaning 'correct', resulting
in 'prove' or 'testify'.

Telling radicals apart

Some of the radicals are extremely similar in appearance. Avoid confusing these:

Radical 74	月	(moon)	
Radical 130	月	(flesh)	The variant form of 肉
Radical 72	日	(sun)	
Radical 73	曰	(say)	
Radical 170	阝	(mound)	Located on the left.
Radical 163	阝	(city)	Located on the right.
Radical 15	冫	(ice)	
Radical 85	氵	(water)	The variant form of 水
Radical 27	厂	(cliff)	
Radical 53	广	(lean-to)	
Radical 104	疒	(disease)	
Radical 8	亠	(cover)	
Radical 40	宀	(roof)	
Radical 116	穴	(cave)	
Radical 22	匚	(basket)	
Radical 23	匸	(box)	
Radical 113	礻	(sign)	
Radical 145	衤	(clothes)	
Radical 169	門	(door)	
Radical 191	鬥	(fight)	

Simplified radicals

Radicals which have been simplified are listed below:

Radical 90	爿 →	丬
Radical 147	見 →	见
Radical 149	言 →	讠
Radical 154	貝 →	贝
Radical 159	車 →	车
Radical 167	金 →	钅
Radical 169	門 →	门
Radical 178	韋 →	韦
Radical 181	頁 →	页
Radical 182	風 →	风
Radical 184	食 →	饣
Radical 187	馬 →	马
Radical 191	鬥 →	门
Radical 195	魚 →	鱼
Radical 196	鳥 →	鸟
Radical 197	鹵 →	卤
Radical 199	麥 →	麦
Radical 205	黽 →	黾
Radical 210	齊 →	齐
Radical 211	齒 →	齿
Radical 212	龍 →	龙
Radical 213	龜 →	龟

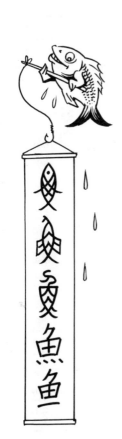

Effects of simplification

What are some of the repercussions of simplification on radicals?

With evolution into the modern simplified form, some changes have taken place.
E.g., the character for 'pig' does not take for its radical 豕 any more. Other examples supplied here also show a change in radical.

Regular form	Simplified form
豬	猪
牆	墙
範	范
護	护
獲	获
雞	鸡
節	节
驚	惊
黴	霉
體	体
響	响
鹽	盐
葉	叶
願	愿
莊	庄

Even more drastic is the fact that some radicals have vanished altogether.

Regular form   **Simplified form**

開術雲滷   开术云卤

開術雲滷   开术云卤

Each of the 214 historical radicals will be enumerated in the complete radical index on pages 20 to 24, and it includes the radical number, variant form, meaning, and one character example.

Because some radicals provide too few or too obscure character examples, it is not possible to analyse each of the 214 radicals individually. Those highlighted warrant attention due to the many useful characters built upon them. An average of 12 examples are given for the major radicals like 'water', 'wood', 'man', 'door', 'speech', etc. For those radicals with fewer relevant examples, an average of 4 have been chosen. Simplifications can be found within brackets.

An explanation follows each character example. Many of these have a whole range of definitions. As the Chinese language is a highly versatile one, a single character very often bears usages and contexts beyond the most obvious and familiar meaning, which is more often than not also the one directly connected to the radical.

Radicals Vol. 1 deals with those radicals which fall under classifications of man, animal, plant and nature, while Vol. 2 carries on with artifacts and implements of man, his actions and characteristics, and finally, numerals and basic strokes.

The Appendix gives a listing of various groups of characters with similar components but different radicals. At a glance it can be seen that with the substitution of a different radical, the character assumes at once a meaning related to it. The listings are by no means exhaustive, and the reader is encouraged to look for other examples, either through the help of the dictionary, or from characters already known.

What to expect

What needs to be stressed at this point is that the radical system is not always the most systematic that one may expect. As there is no hard and fast rule, irregularities do occur. So there should not be too many hairs split over why 辦 comes under the radical 辛 and yet 瓣 is found under the radical 瓜 .

Another area of complexity is where a character having no apparent connection to the radical is nevertheless listed under it! All these defy analysis and have, alas, to be accepted as the freaks of lexicography.

No.		Pinyin	Meaning	Example
1	一	yī	one	下
2	丨			中
3	、			主
4	丿			之
5	乙	yǐ		乾
6	亅		hook	事
7	二	èr	two	些
8	亠		cover	亮
9	人(亻)	rén	man	住
10	儿		man (legs)	兄
11	入	rù	to enter	內
12	八	bā	eight	其
13	冂		borders	再
14	冖		crown	冠
15	冫		ice	凍
16	几	jī	table	凱
17	凵		bowl	凶
18	刀(刂)	dāo	knife	割
19	力	lì	strength	動
20	勹		wrap	包
21	匕		ladle	化
22	匚		basket	匠
23	匸		box	匹
24	十	shí	ten	升
25	卜	bǔ	divine	卦
26	卩		seal	印
27	厂		cliff	原
28	厶		cocoon	去
29	又	yòu	right hand	友
30	口	kǒu	mouth	喊
31	囗		enclosure	圍
32	土	tǔ	earth	地
33	士	shì	scholar	壽
34	夂		follow	夆
35	夊		slow	夏
36	夕	xī	dusk	夜
37	大	dà	big	奪
38	女	nǚ	woman	娘
39	子	zǐ	son	存
40	宀		roof	宿
41	寸	cùn	inch	對
42	小	xiǎo	little	少

43	尤(尣，兀)		lame	就
44	尸	shī	corpse	尾
45	屮		sprout	屯
46	山	shān	mountain	岸
47	川(巛)	chuān	river	州
48	工	gōng	work	差
49	己	jǐ	self	巷
50	巾	jīn	cloth	帽
51	干	gān	shield	平
52	幺	yāo	slender	幾
53	广		lean-to	店
54	廴		march	建
55	廾		clasp	弄
56	弋	yì	dart	式
57	弓	gōng	bow	張
58	彐(彑，彐)		pig's head	彙
59	彡		streaks	彰
60	彳	chì	step	從
61	心(忄，⺗)	xīn	heart	急
62	戈	gē	lance	戰
63	戶	hù	door	房
64	手(扌)	shǒu	hand	捉
65	支	zhī	branch	支
66	攴(攵)		knock	放
67	文	wén	literature	爛
68	斗	dǒu	scoop	料
69	斤	jīn	axe	新
70	方	fāng	square	施
71	无	wú	lack	既
72	日	rì	sun	明
73	曰	yuē	to say	會
74	月	yuè	moon	期
75	木	mù	wood	桌
76	欠	qiàn	to yawn	欺
77	止	zhǐ	to stop	步
78	歹	dǎi	bad	殘
79	殳	shū	kill	毀
80	毋(母)		do not!	每
81	比	bǐ	to compare	毗
82	毛	máo	fur	毯
83	氏	shì	clan	民
84	气	qì	breath	氣

21

#	Character	Pinyin	Meaning	
85	水(氵, 水)	shuǐ	water	滑
86	火(灬)	huǒ	fire	煮
87	爪(爫)	zhǎo	claw	爭
88	父	fù	father	爸
89	爻	yáo	crisscross	爽
90	爿	bàn	plank	牀
91	片	piàn	slice	版
92	牙	yá	tooth	牚
93	牛(牜)	niú	cow	物
94	犬(犭)	quǎn	dog	獵
95	玄	xuán	dark	率
96	玉(王)	yù	jade	珠
97	瓜	guā	melon	瓠
98	瓦	wǎ	tile	瓶
99	甘	gān	sweet	甜
100	生	shēng	produce	產
101	用	yòng	use	甬
102	田	tian	field	番
103	疋	pī	roll of cloth	疑
104	疒		disease	痛
105	癶		back	發
106	白	bái	white	皇
107	皮	pí	skin	皺
108	皿	mǐn	vessel	盤
109	目	mù	eye	眠
110	矛	máo	spear	矞
111	矢	shǐ	arrow	短
112	石	shí	rock	硬
113	示(礻)	shì	sign	神
114	禸		track	禺
115	禾	hé	grain	種
116	穴	xué	cave	窗
117	立	lì	stand	站
118	竹(⺮)	zhú	bamboo	筆
119	米	mǐ	rice	粒
120	糸		silk	織
121	缶	fǒu	earthenware	罐
122	网(罒, 罓)		net	罪
123	羊(⺷, 羋)	yáng	sheep	羣
124	羽	yǔ	feather	耀
125	老	lǎo	old	考
126	而	ér	yet	耐
127	耒	lěi	plough	耘

22

128	耳	ěr	ear	聲
129	聿	yù	brush	肆
130	肉(月)	ròu	flesh	脚
131	臣	chén	official	臨
132	自	zì	self	臭
133	至	zhì	reach	致
134	臼	jiù	mortar	舉
135	舌	shé	tongue	舒
136	舛		discord	舞
137	舟	zhōu	boat	船
138	艮	gèn	stubborn	艱
139	色	sè	colour	艷
140	艸(艹)	cǎo	grass	芳
141	虍		tiger	處
142	虫	chóng	insect	蝦
143	血	xuè	blood	蟻
144	行	xíng	go	衝
145	衣(衤)	yī	clothing	裙
146	西(襾)	xī	west	要
147	見	jiàn	see	親
148	角	jiǎo	horn	解
149	言	yán	speech	語
150	谷	gǔ	valley	谿
151	豆	dòu	bean	豐
152	豕	shǐ	pig	象
153	豸	zhì	cat	貌
154	貝	bèi	money	財
155	赤	chì	raw	赦
156	走	zǒu	walk	趕
157	足	zú	foot	跑
158	身	shēn	body	躺
159	車	chē	vehicle	輪
160	辛	xīn	bitter	辦
161	辰	chén	time	農
162	辵(辶)		halt	迎
163	邑(阝)	yì	city	部
164	酉		wine	醉
165	釆		separate	釋
166	里	lǐ	mile	野
167	金	jīn	gold	鐵
168	長	cháng	long	長
169	門	mén	door	關
170	阜(阝)	fù	mound	院

23

171	隶		reach	隸
172	隹		short-tailed bird	雄
173	雨	yǔ	rain	雷
174	青	qīng	green	靜
175	非	fēi	not	靠
176	面	miàn	face	靦
177	革	gé	leather	鞋
178	韋	wéi	leather	韓
179	韭	jiǔ	leeks	韭
180	音	yīn	sound	響
181	頁	yè	head	頂
182	風	fēng	wind	颭
183	飛	fēi	fly	飛
184	食	shí	food	餅
185	首	shǒu	chief	馘
186	香	xiāng	fragrance	馥
187	馬	mǎ	horse	騎
188	骨	gǔ	bone	體
189	高	gāo	tall	高
190	髟		hair	鬆
191	鬥	dòu	fight	鬧
192	鬯	chàng	sacrificial wine	鬱
193	鬲		cauldron	鬻
194	鬼	guǐ	demon	魂
195	魚	yú	fish	鮮
196	鳥	niǎo	bird	鵝
197	鹵	lǔ	salt	鹹
198	鹿	lù	deer	麗
199	麥	mài	wheat	麵
200	麻	má	hemp	麼
201	黃	huáng	yellow	黊
202	黍	shǔ	millet	黏
203	黑	hēi	black	默
204	黹	zhǐ	embroider	黼
205	黽	mǐn	try	鼈
206	鼎	dǐng	tripod	鼐
207	鼓	gǔ	drum	鼟
208	鼠	shǔ	mouse	鼯
209	鼻	bí	nose	鼾
210	齊	qí	harmony	齋
211	齒	chǐ	teeth	齡
212	龍	lóng	dragon	龔
213	龜	guī	tortoise	龜
214	龠	yuè	flute	龥

THINGS

衣	宀	舟	匕
糸	一	斤	酉
巾	瓦	干	皿
貝	广	戈	斗
門	网	弓	臼
戶	耒	刀	缶
片	車	矢	卩
	聿		

yī

clothing

衤

Individual items of clothing and attire like gowns, jackets, trousers, skirts, socks and stockings all take the 'clothing' radical. Sleeves, though not worn separately, and lining, which should be invisible, are parts of clothing, and belong to the same radical family.

袖

袖 xiù
Sleeve.

袍 páo
Robe, gown.

裁 cái
To cut, to trim; to reduce; decision, judgement.

裙 qún
Skirt.

補

補（补）bǔ
To repair, to patch; to make up; to nourish.

裝（装）zhuāng
To dress up; to pretend; to load; to install, fix.

製（制）zhì
To make, to create; to produce, to manufacture.

裙

褲（裤）kù
Trousers, pants.

襖（袄）ǎo
Coat, jacket.

襪（袜）wà
Socks; stockings.

褂 guà
Outer jacket, a coat.

裏（里）lǐ
Inside; lining.

裂 liè
Crack; tear; rip.

被 bèi
Quilt, blanket; to cover, to wear; by (indicating the passive voice).

裂

糸 **silk**

糸(糹)

RADICAL 120

The 'silk' radical 糸, which resembles a skein of silk, is responsible for a whole host of characters. Among these are rope or string (繩), thread or wire (綫), web (網), and various characters meaning 'bind' or 'fasten'. Weave, knit, sew, and embroider – making fabric or items out of fibre or yarn – are other relevant examples.

紙(纸) zhǐ
Paper.

綁(绑) bǎng
Tie, bind, fasten together.

絲(丝) sī
Silk.

繡(绣) xiù
Embroider.

緊

緊(紧) jǐn
Tight; urgent.

綿(绵) mián
Floss silk; soft; continuous.

網(网) wǎng
Net; web; network.

綫(线) xiàn
Thread; filament; wire.

縫(缝) féng
Sew, stitch; mend, patch.

織(织) zhī
Knit; weave.

網

繞(绕) rào
Coil, entwine; revolve; make a detour.

繫(系) xì
Tie up; fasten.

編

編(编) biān
Braid, to plait; to weave, to knit; arrange; edit, compile.

繼(继) jì
Continue, succeed, follow after.

繭(茧) jiǎn
The cocoon of a silkworm.

jīn

cloth

RADICAL 50

Flags, banners, tents, streamers, sails, curtains and screens – which generally require large expanses of cloth, issue from this radical. In ancient times, notices and announcements were written on scrolls, giving rise to the character 帖 . Smaller personal items like belt (帶), handkerchief (帕) and hat (帽) are included as well.

帕

帕　pà
A turban; a handkerchief.

帷　wéi
Curtain.

幅　fú
The width of cloth; a roll (of paper); a scroll (of painting).

帐

帽

幕

布　bù
Cloth; arrange; publish, make known.

帆　fān
Sail, canvas.

帖　tiě
Invitation card; notice.

席　xí
Straw or bamboo mat; seat; banquet.

帐(帐)　zhàng
Tent; mosquito net; a scroll sent to mourners.

帽　mào
Hat, cap.

幕　mù
Tent; stage curtain or screen; movie screen; act of a play.

帜(帜)　zhì
A flag; a banner.

幡　fān
Streamers hung before a shrine.

帮(帮)　bāng
To help; a group, a party.

31

貝 （贝）

money

RADICAL 154

Money, a most valuable asset, functions as a common radical. It features in characters like wealth (財), spending it (費), gambling it away (賭), earning it (賺), winning it (贏), a thief who steals it away (賊), buy and sell (買賣), expensive (貴), and the result of consumption – a bill (賬)!

販

財（财）cái
Property; wealth, valuables.

貨（货）huò
Goods, merchandise.

貪（贪）tān
Greedy, covetous.

販（贩）fàn
Buy and sell, trade; a peddler, a hawker.

費（费）fèi
Expenditure; spend, use, consume; waste.

貴（贵）guì
Expensive; honourable; noble.

資（资）zī
Wealth, property, capital; to give, to provide; aptitude; qualifications.

賊（贼）zéi
A thief, a burglar; a rebel, an enemy; undesirable person.

賞（赏）shǎng
Bestow, grant; reward; enjoy, appreciate.

賬（账）zhàng
Account, bill.

賜（赐）cì
Bestow, grant.

賭（赌）dǔ
Gamble, make a bet.

賺（赚）zhuàn
To earn, to gain, to make (money).

贏（赢）yíng
Win; score.

貴

賊

$1/- $2/-

贏

門 (门)　mén

door

RADICAL 169

Being an entrance as well as a frame constructed to impede entry, the door operates as the radical in such characters as open (開) and close (關, 閉, 闔). There are other ways of opening up – disclosure (闡) and penetration (闢). And as for forced entry the character shows, amusingly, a horse in the doorway (闖).

 闖

閃(闪)　shǎn
A flash of light; avoid; sparkle.

闢(辟)　pì
To open up; to refute.

闔(盍)　hé
All, whole; shut, close.

闖(闯)　chuǎng
To force one's way, to rush, to break through.

34

閑

閉（闭）bì
To shut; to obstruct.

閑（闲）xián
Unoccupied, free.

開（开）kāi
To open, to start.

關（关）guān
Close, shut; a frontier gate, a pass; customs station; a turning point; involve.

閉

閨（闺）guī
A small door; a boudoir.

闌（阑）lán
Railing; block; nearly finished or completed.

閎（闳）hóng
Great, large.

開

閣（阁）gé
A chamber; a pavilion; the cabinet.

闕（阙）què
The gate tower of an imperial palace.

闡（阐）chǎn
To express; to disclose; to enlighten.

户

hù

door

户

RADICAL 63

This radical also means 'door', but shows only one side of the door. It has fewer examples, although they are relevant ones. 所 is the general character for place, including offices and departments like clinic (診療所), research department (研究所), community centre (聯絡所), etc. 房 is of course house or room.

扇

扇 shān
To fan; stir, agitate.

所 suǒ
A place; an office, a centre.

房 fáng
House or apartment; room, chamber.

扁 biǎn
Flat.

36

片

piàn

slice

RADICAL 91

Make no mistake, too many pieces of paper can baffle the sense. Similarly, not taking the trouble to read signs properly could prove a pain in the behind. 片 is the radical meaning 'slice' or 'piece'. Most of the handful of characters with this radical are given below.

牌

版 bǎn
A register; a block for printing; an edition; a newspaper page.

牌 pái
Board; tablet or card (for advertisements, signs, notices, etc.).

牘(牘) dú
A note, a letter, a document.

roof

RADICAL 40

Everything under one roof – with a domestic animal like the pig one gets a home (家), with a woman one keeps the peace (安), with prized possessions like porcelain, money and jade there is treasure (寶). The roof provides shelter, and lodging (室) is therefore arrival (至) under a roof (宀).

家

宮 gōng
The palace; an ancestral temple.

家 jiā
A household, a family; a school (of learning); a specialist.

密 mì
Close together, dense; closely related, intimate; secret; precise.

寶

富 fù
Wealthy; abundant.

寒 hán
Cold, chilly; poor, needy.

寡 guǎ
Few, scant; a widow.

寶（宝） bǎo
Treasure; precious, valuable; highly prized.

守

宿 sù
Lodging; long-standing.

守 shǒu
To guard, to defend; to abide by; wait.

安 ān
Calm, quiet; safe; to pacify; to install.

安

定 dìng
Tranquil, stable, fixed; to determine, to decide; firm; order, arrange; surely, certainly.

客 kè
Guest, visitor; passenger, customer.

室 shì
House, room; office; restaurant.

cover

RADICAL 8

Though the 'cover' radical resembles the 'roof' radical somewhat, it looks more like a lid, without the two eaves which protrude from the edges of the 'roof'. There is no apparent connection between the radical and its character examples, except perhaps in pavilion or shelter (亭) and capital (京).

亭

交 jiāo
Deliver, hand over; acquaint, befriend; intersect.

亭 tíng
A pavilion; a kiosk, a shelter.

亮 liàng
Bright, clear; elucidate; loud and clear.

瓦 wǎ

tile

RADICAL 98

Earthenware and crockery like jars, vases and urns, and bottles, pitchers and jugs can be seen to bear the same radical. More precious and fragile porcelain and chinaware belong here too.

甕

瓶 píng
Bottle, jar, pitcher, jug, vase.

瓷 cí
Porcelain.

甄 zhēn
Examine; distinguish.

甕（瓮） wèng
Urn; earthen jar.

广

lean-to

Another shelter radical, this one is like a roof seen from the side. Here, the examples do relate to particular places like the verandah (廊), living room area (廳), block of apartments or mansion (厦), factory (廠), kitchen (厨), etc. However, the dot has been removed in some simplifications.

底

底 dǐ
Bottom, base; below; the end; a draft; reach.

店 diàn
A shop, a store; an inn, a tavern.

座 zuò
Seat; measure word for mountain, bridge, tall building, reservoir, etc.

厨

廈 shà
A tall building;
mansion.

廊 láng
Porch; corridor;
verandah.

厨 chú
A kitchen.

廳(厅) tīng
A living room; a
parlour; a dining room.

庭

厠(厕) cè
A toilet, a lavatory.

廢(废) fèi
Cancel, discontinue;
spoilt, worthless, waste.

庭 tíng
A courtyard; a court of
justice.

廂 xiāng
A side-room; a suburb;
a compartment.

廈

廣(广) guǎng
Wide, extensive, broad,
spacious; common,
popular; expand, spread.

廠(广) chǎng
A factory; a plant; a
workhouse.

网 net

RADICAL 122

Evil deeds and wrongdoing will have their just deserts. Punishment (罰), for instance, is inflicted upon the criminal or offender, and for his wrong deed (非), the evildoer is trapped in his guilt and suffering.

罪

罔 wǎng
Deceive; nothing.

罪 zuì
A crime, offence; guilt; suffering.

罸(罚) fá
Punish, fine, forfeit.

置 zhì
To place, to put; arrange, install; buy.

44

lěi

plough

RADICAL 127

The work of ploughing the fields for cultivation of crops (耕), weeding (耘), and implements needed to facilitate such a labour like the rake or harrow (耙) are obviously linked. Their common denominator is the 'plough' radical, which supplies the meaning to all these characters.

耕

耗　hào
Waste time, squander; consume; bad news, information.

耘　yún
To weed.

耙(耙)　bà
A rake; a harrow.

耕　gēng
Plough, cultivate.

車 （车）

chē

vehicle

RADICAL 159

Under the 'car' or 'vehicle' radical are various characters for carriage like 輦, 軫 and 轎; also, parts of the wheel, which keep the vehicle in motion. Its appearance in characters like transport or carry (載) makes the meaning even more apparent. Perhaps the most graphic example is the character for rumble or explode (轟), where three cars are involved in a pile-up!

轟

轟（轰） hōng
Bang, crash, roar (of thunder or any explosive noise); bombard.

軍（军） jūn
An army; troops; soldiers; corps.

輕（轻） qīng
Light; minor; pay scant attention to; hasty.

輪

輛（辆）liàng
A measure word for vehicles.

輪（轮）lún
A wheel; a gear.

輻（辐）fú
Spokes of a wheel.

輸（输）shū
Transport, convey; lose, be defeated.

轆

轆（辘）lù
A pulley; wheel and axle; a windlass; the rumbling of carriages.

輳（辏）còu
The hub of a wheel.

轄（辖）xiá
The linchpin of a wheel; govern, control.

載

輾（辗）zhǎn
To roll; turn over.

轉（转）zhuǎn
To revolve; to rotate, to turn, to change; to transfer.

載（载）zài
To load, to carry, to transport; to fill with.

zhōu

舟

boat

RADICAL 137

The 'boat' radical is positioned consistently on the left side of the character, and is always a direct clue to the meaning. Here can be found seaworthy vessels of various shapes and sizes, from the formidable warship down to the modest sampan. About the only odd one out is 般, having no connection to boats, ships, or the sea.

航

航 háng
A boat; a large vessel; sail; fly (a plane).

舰（舰）jiàn
Warship; naval vessel; man-of-war.

舵 duò
Rudder; helm.

船

船　chuán
A boat, a ship; any floating vessel.

艘　sōu
Numeral for ships and vessels.

舳　zhú
Stern of a ship.

艙（舱）　cāng
The hold of a ship or an aeroplane.

艇

艇　tǐng
A light boat; a canoe; a punt, a barge.

舶　bó
Oceangoing ship.

舢板　shānbǎn
Sampan.

舷

舷　xián
The side of a ship; the bulwarks; the gunwale.

舫　fǎng
A boat, a vessel.

般　bān
Sort, kind, class, manner.

jīn

axe

RADICAL 69

Although the meaning of this character is 'a unit of weight', the radical is derived from the character 斧 or axe. It is therefore no accident that 'to chop off' or 'to cut in two' (斬) and 'to cut' or 'to break off' (斷) have this particular radical.

斬

斧 fǔ
An axe, a hatchet.

斬(斩) zhǎn
To chop off, to cut in two.

斷(断) duàn
Cut off, break off; discontinue.

50

干 gān

shield

干 was the ancient character for 'shield'. Unfortunately, no connection can be drawn based on the mere handful of examples. The only exception to this is 幹, which means 'do' or 'manage', or 'skilful' or 'able'. Incidentally, its simplified character is none other than 干.

幹

平 píng
Flat, smooth; fair; peaceful; ordinary.

幸 xìng
Fortunate.

并 bìng
Combine; and.

幹(干) gàn
Trunk; make, manage; skilful, able.

51

戈

gē

lance

RADICAL 62

Ancient warriors never advanced into battle without being armed with the necessary weaponry, hence this 'lance' radical accounts for characters like 戎 (military), 戰 (war), 戡 (suppress), 截 (intercept), 戳 (pierce), and 戮 (slaughter).

戎　róng
Military; army.

戰(战) zhàn
War, battle; to fight; to tremble, to quiver.

戒　jiè
Take precaution, guard against; give up (a habit).

戓

成　chéng
To finish, to accomplish; to become; to win, to succeed.

戡　kān
Suppress or subdue; to put down.

戚　qī
Relative; sorrow.

截　jié
Cut; intercept, stop.

戍　shù
Guard, defend.

戲(戏)　xì
Play; game; make fun of; theatrical performance, drama, play.

戲

戴　dài
Wear, bear; respect, support.

戳

戳　chuō
To poke, to pierce; stamp, seal.

戮　lù
Kill, stab, slaughter, put to death.

gōng

bow

RADICAL 57

 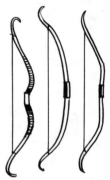

In archery, the string of the bow has to be stretched as far back as possible to release the arrow. This explains therefore the presence of the 'bow' radical in characters like 張 (expand, stretch), 弘 (expand, enlarge), 引 (stretch), and 彎 (bend). Shooting a catapult requires a similar skill, hence 彈 .

引

引 yǐn
Draw (a bow); stretch; guide, lead; to refer to.

弘 hóng
Great, expanded; to expand, to enlarge.

弭 mǐ
To stop; to check.

弦

弦　xián
The elastic cord on a bow; musical chord; a crescent moon.

弩　nǔ
A crossbow.

弱　ruò
Weak, feeble.

彈

彈(弹)　tán
To flick, to flip; to shoot, to snap; to spring, to bounce.

張(张)　zhāng
To open up; to stretch; to expand, to look; a measure word for leaf, sheet, piece, etc.

強　qiáng
Strong and healthy; forcefully; firm.

彌(弥)　mí
Full, whole; to make up, to amend.

彎

彎(弯)　wān
Draw a bow; bent, curved, arched; bend, turn.

刀 dāo

knife

刂

RADICAL 18

More often than not, the 'knife' radical appears in its variant form on the character's right side. The sharpness of the knife blade (利) is useful not only in cutting, chopping, dividing; frequent references to sharp tongues have proven that knives are not the only instruments with potent cutting edges!

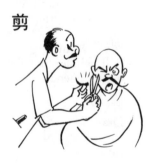

剛（刚）gāng
Solid, hard, firm, unyielding; just, recently.

剪 jiǎn
Shears, scissors; cut, chop, shear.

割 gē
Cut, sever, divide.

切 qiē
Cut, chop.

利

分　fēn
Divide, separate;
distribute, distinguish;
portion, part.

利　lì
Sharp, acute;
advantageous, useful;
smooth-going.

劃（划）　huà
Draw, classify, divide;
plan, planning.

刻

刻　kè
To carve, to engrave;
harsh.

劍（剑）　jiàn
A sword, a dagger.

初　chū
At first; beginning.

判　pàn
Divide, differentiate;
judge, decide.

刺

別　bié
Leave, depart; classify,
distinguish; another; do
not.

刺　cì
A thorn, a sting, a
prick; to pierce, to
thrust, to stab.

矢 shǐ

arrow

RADICAL 111

Unlike the 'bow' radical, the 'arrow' radical's examples are scant. Two of the more common examples happen to be 短 (short, referring to something inanimate), and 矮 (short, this time in reference to a person). Neither is related to the arrow in any way.

矮

知 zhī
Know, perceive, be aware.

矩 jǔ
A rule, a law, a pattern.

短 duǎn
Short; lacking.

矮 ǎi
Short; low in rank or position.

匕

ladle

RADICAL 21

Another radical which works in mysterious ways, it has given rise to characters of widely different meanings. Transform or alter (化), north (北), and spoon (匙) come arbitrarily under the same radical, though only spoon bears any relation to the radical.

化 huà
Change, alter, transform; dissolve, melt.

北 běi
North.

匙 chí
A spoon.

酉

wine

RADICAL 164

Wine is a necessary ingredient at social gatherings. Thus, when one entertains or attends a social function, one is said to 'pledge with wine' (應酬). Vinegar (醋) is made from beer or weak wine, and the Chinese expression of 'eating vinegar' connotes jealousy. The 'wine' radical is also prominent in characters for 'drunken' and 'sober' states.

吃醋

酸　suān
Sour; grieved, sad; ache due to overfatigue or illness.

酬　chóu
To pledge with wine, to entertain; to repay, to reward.

醋　cù
Vinegar; jealousy.

酣　hān
Merry from drinking; rapturous.

酒　jiǔ
Liquor, wine, spirit.

配　pèi
To matchmake; to blend, to compose; worth, fit.

醉　zuì
To be drunk.

酷　kù
Cruel, harsh, oppressive; very, extremely.

酤　gū
Wine; buy or sell wine.

醜(丑)　chǒu
Ugly; disgraceful, shameful.

醬(酱)　jiàng
Soy sauce; gravy.

醒　xǐng
Awake, sober; awaken, come to realize.

酥　sū
Crispy; soft, tender; butter, cheese.

mǐn

vessel

RADICAL 108

A vessel or receptacle of some sort, this radical invariably appears at the bottom of the character. The types of receptacle vary from basins and tubs to plates, dishes and trays, even boxes. As for 盛 , which means 'luxuriant', 'flourishing', the combination of 成 and 皿 no doubt suggests that one's plate is filled abundantly.

盆 pén
A basin; a pot; a tub.

盈 yíng
Be full of, be filled with; a surplus of.

盏(盞) zhǎn
Small cup; measure word for lamp or cup.

盒 hé
Box, casket, carton.

62

盛

盛 shèng
Luxuriant, prosperous, flourishing; strong, grand, splendid; widely, to a great extent.

盎 àng
An ancient vessel with a big belly and a small mouth.

盡(尽) jìn
Completed, finished; the utmost, the last; fulfil.

盤

盤(盘) pán
A plate, a dish, a tray; to circle around; in detail; expenses.

監(监) jiān
Examine carefully, supervise; a prison, a jail.

盒

盥 guàn
Wash (the hands or face).

益 yì
Benefit, profit, advantage; increase.

盂 yú
A broad-mouthed receptacle for holding liquid.

dǒu

scoop

RADICAL 68

Seeing that this radical means 'a peck measure' or 'scoop', referring therefore to the measurement of grain, it is present in the following handful of examples. In fact, the radical is itself a pictograph of a scoop – with the stroke sloping downwards, and the two dots resembling two grains.

料 liào
Raw materials; grain; suppose, guess.

斜 xié
Slanting, inclining; sloping; oblique.

斟 zhēn
To pour out.

64

臼 jiù

mortar

RADICAL 134

𦥑

A variant form of the 'mortar' radical manifests itself in 舉 (raise, hold up), and similarly in 與 (and, with; give; help; intimate) and 興 (launch, establish; interest).

舉

舀 yǎo
To bale out water; to dip.

舊(旧) jiù
Old, ancient; worn, second-hand.

舉(举) jǔ
Raise, lift, hold up; praise; behaviour; begin, inaugurate; cite.

缶 fǒu

earthenware

RADICAL 121

Earthen vessels and jars carry the 'earthenware' radical, and it is interesting to find that characters meaning 'deficient', 'lacking', 'having a shortcoming', like 缺 and 罅 have the same radical too. The original meaning of 缺 is 'broken' and 罅 is 'crack' or 'rift'.

罐

缸 gāng
Earthen vessel; jar.

罐 guàn
Can; pot; tin.

缺 quē
Lack; incomplete; a vacancy; absent.

罌(甖) yīng
Jar; vase.

口

seal

RADICAL 26

In shape, the 'seal' radical is evolved from the ancient seal script of a kneeling figure. Among the characters with this radical are 印 (seal, stamp), and 卷 (book, volume). In addition, 危 (perilous, dangerous, critical) is another example.

卷

印 yìn
A seal, a rubber-stamp; trace; print; tally with.

卸 xiè
Unload; dismantle; get rid of.

卷 juàn
A book, a volume; test paper; a volume (measure word).

聿

yù

brush

RADICAL 129

Calligraphy is an art requiring much discipline and control, so with this radical – derived from the action of a hand holding up a writing brush firmly – we get characters meaning 'study' (肄) and 'solemn' or 'serious' (肅).

肅

肄 yì
Study.

肆 sì
Reckless, unrestrained.

肅(肃) sù
Respectful, solemn;
stern, majestic, serious.

肇 zhào
To occur, to cause.

ACTIONS

見	日	彳	口
欠	立	走	止
食	工	行	示
言	疋	殳	攴

勹

見 （见）

jiàn

see

RADICAL 147

Looking at, viewing, examining, inspecting – are possible because of the faculty of vision. Thus characters representing these acts of seeing carry the 'to see' radical. One most fascinating example is 'covet' (覬), which means, literally, 'to cast one's greedy eyes on'. And 展覽會 is an exhibition, a display meant for public viewing.

 觀

規（规） guī
Law, rule, regulation; plan; advise, warn.

視（视） shì
Regard, consider; see, look; inspect, examine.

覥见 tiǎn
Shy, timid.

親

覩（觌）dǔ
To see.

親（亲）qīn
Parents; related by blood or marriage; personal; close, dear, intimate; to kiss.

覬（觊）jì
Covet.

覯（觏）gòu
See, meet.

覺

觀（观）guān
Look at, view, inspect; a view, a sight; an opinion or viewpoint.

覺（觉）jiào
Sleep, nap.

覺（觉）jué
Sense; feel, perceive; be aware of, understand, realize.

覽（览）lǎn
See, sightsee, view; read.

覽

欠

qiàn

to yawn

RADICAL 76

Meaning 'to yawn', the original seal character shows a person yawning with mouth wide open. As the mouth is involved in laughing and crying and singing, this radical occurs in characters like 欣 (glad), 歡 (pleased), 歌 (song), and 欷 (sigh).

歔 xū
Sob in secret.

欷 xī
Sob; sigh.

歡 (欢) huān
Jolly, cheerful, pleased.

欺

次 cì
Order, position; inferior; a time (measure word); a place.

欺 qī
Cheat, deceive, fool; bully, insult, abuse.

歉

欣 xīn
Happy, glad, delighted.

欲 yù
Desire, wish, hope; need; about to, going to (happen).

款 kuǎn
Sincere; entertain; sum of money, fund.

歌

歇 xiē
Rest; stop.

歉 qiàn
Bad harvest; sorry, regretful.

歌 gē
Song, ballad; to sing.

73

食 shí

food

RADICAL 184

飠(饣)

People eat for basic survival as well as for pleasure, and as a radical, it is common to many characters. Being full (飽) and hungry (餓), nourish (養), meal (餐), are significant examples. Individual types of food also carry the 'food' radical, these being the staple of rice (飯), biscuit or cake (餅), dumpling (餃) and bun (饅).

飽

養(养) yǎng
To raise, bring up; to support; to rear; convalesce, nourish; cultivate.

飽(饱) bǎo
To be full, satiated.

飯(饭) fàn
Cooked rice; a meal.

餅

飲(饮) yǐn
Drink.

餅(饼) bǐng
Cake, pastry, biscuit.

餐 cān
A meal.

餓(饿) è
Hungry, starved.

餓

饑(饥) jī
Hungry, insufficient;
famine.

館(馆) guǎn
A hotel, a restaurant; a
hall; a commercial
service centre.

饅(馒) mán
Steamed bread or bun.

餞(饯) jiàn
Give a farewell party.

餘

餘(余) yú
Remainder, surplus;
beyond, after.

饒(饶) ráo
Abundant, plentiful,
resourceful; to spare, to
forgive.

yán

speech

言（讠）

RADICAL 149

Although the faculty of speech can be used to advantage – to thank, to educate, to caution, to invite, etc., abuse leads to idle talk, lying, swearing, boasting, and other undesirable acts. The very common 'speech' radical mostly occurs on the left side; whenever it appears at the bottom, it is not simplified.

討論

討論（讨论）　tǎolùn
To discuss; to talk over.

訪（访）　fǎng
Call upon, visit; enquire into, search for.

誓　shì
Swear, vow, make an oath.

詩（诗）　shī
Poetry, poem, verse.

誇(夸) kuā
Praise, extol; boast, brag.

請(请) qǐng
Request, ask for; invite; a courteous word meaning 'please'.

誦(诵) sòng
Recite, read out loud; praise.

謊(谎) huǎng
Lie, falsehood.

講(讲) jiǎng
Talk, converse; explain.

謝(谢) xiè
Express gratitude, thank; apologise; decline, reject; wither, fade.

談(谈) tán
To speak, to converse; gossip, chat.

謠(谣) yáo
Folk song, ballad, rhymes; rumour.

警 jǐng
Notify, caution, warn; police; an emergency.

77

曰 yuē

to say

RADICAL 73

The radical 'to say' is truly more of a mystery. There is remarkably little to say about it, except for 'verses' (曲) and 'meeting' or 'assembly' (會), which does require verbal participation.

曲

曲 qǔ
Song, lyrics; classical Chinese verses.

更 gēng
Alter, change; night watch.

書（书） shū
Book; calligraphy, writing; document, certificate; letter.

曼 màn
Graceful, fine, handsome; long, prolonged.

曹 cáo
A company, a class, a generation.

替 tì
To substitute, to replace; on behalf of.

曾 céng
Already; at some time in the past.

最 zuì
Most, best, to the highest degree.

曳 yè
Drag, haul, tug, tow.

會（会） huì
Assemble, meet together; association, society; able to.

立 lì

stand

RADICAL 117

A person standing with both arms raised and legs astride is the way the character was originally represented in its seal form. 'To stand' (站) is therefore directly related to the radical, and in 'compete' or 'contend' (競), there are two males (兄) standing side by side in competition.

競

站 zhàn
To stand; station or stop (as in railway station or bus stop).

競 (竞) jìng
Compete, contend, strive.

端 duān
Proper, decent, direct; to carry.

gōng

work

RADICAL 48

To say the least, the following examples show a set of vastly different characters all nevertheless belonging to the same radical family of 'work'. Perhaps 'witchcraft' (巫) is similar to being 'ingenious' and 'cunning' (巧) in that both require a special craft or skill.

巧

巧 qiǎo
Skilful, ingenious, clever; cunning, deceitful; coincidentally.

巨 jù
Huge, tremendous, gigantic.

巫 wū
Shaman, witch, wizard.

halt

RADICAL 162

This radical is only seen in its variant form. The idea of journeying forth and a passage is present in most of the character examples, even if sometimes it is in pursuit (追), to escape from (逃), or being lost (迷). Meeting, greeting and arriving and concepts of distance like far (遠) and near (近) have the same radical too.

過(过) guò
Cross, pass; across, over; spend time; after; exceed; fault, mistake.

道 dào
Road, path; channel; way, method.

達(达) dá
Extend; reach; understand thoroughly; express, communicate.

遲

82

追 zhuī
Chase, pursue; trace, get to the bottom of; seek; recall.

逃 táo
Escape, run away from; evade, shirk.

途 tú
Way, road, route.

遇 yù
Meet; receive; chance, opportunity.

迎 yíng
Greet, welcome; move towards, meet head-on.

進(进) jìn
Advance, move forward; enter; receive.

遲(迟) chí
Slow, tardy.

迷 mí
Be confused; be lost; be fascinated by; fan of, enthusiast of.

遠(远) yuǎn
Far, distant, remote.

近 jìn
Close, near.

chì

step

RADICAL 60

A radical with less examples to its credit than 辶 , it has nonetheless some characters of significance like 循 and 從 (follow), 往 (head towards), 還 (come back), and 徘徊 (pace), as anxious fathers are wont to do in ward corridors!

徒

徹（彻） chè
Thorough, penetrating.

徐 xú
Slowly, gently.

徒 tú
On foot; empty, bare; merely, only; in vain; apprentice, disciple.

循 xún
Follow, abide by.

徘徊

征 zhēng
Go on a journey, or an expedition; be drafted; collect, levy (taxes); ask for, solicit; sign, evidence.

律 lǜ
Law, statute, rule; restrain.

徘徊 páihuí
Pace up and down; hesitate, waver.

後(后) hòu
Behind, back; after, later.

復(复) fù
Turn around; answer; recover, resume; revenge; again.

德 dé
Virtue, morals; heart, mind; kindness, favour.

徑(径) jìng
Footpath, path, track; way, means; directly, diameter.

御 yù
Drive (a carriage); imperial; resist, keep out, ward off.

走

zǒu

walk

走

RADICAL 156

Walking can be anything from a leisurely stroll to a brisk trot, or a walk almost like a run as in big walk contests. As such, the 'walk' radical includes the characters for 'overtake' (超) and 'hasten' (趕). Getting up from one's prostrate position on the bed (起) also means that one has to start walking about and administer the day's affairs.

趣

趨(趍) qū
Hasten, hurry along; tend towards, tend to become.

趣 qù
Interest, delight; interesting.

赴 fù
Go to, attend.

超 chāo
Exceed, surpass, overtake; ultra-, super-, extra-; transcend, go beyond.

趟 tàng
A measure word (e.g. one trip).

赳 jiū
Valiant, gallant.

超

起 qǐ
Take up; set out, get up.

趁 chèn
Take advantage of; while, take the opportunity to (do something).

越 yuè
Get over, jump over; exceed, overstep; loud and strong, at a high pitch (describing voice or emotion).

起

趕

趕(赶) gǎn
Catch up with, overtake; make a dash for; hurry through; drive away.

xíng

go

RADICAL 144

The 'go' radical is similar to the 'step' radical in appearance, except for the addition of the component on the right hand side. The radical 行 is stretched, and the middle element, which always varies, will then produce a different character.

衛

街 jiē
Street.

衝(冲) chōng
Hastily, hurriedly.

衛(卫) wèi
Defend, guard, protect.

殳 **kill**

RADICAL 79

Some of the common examples listed under this radical happen to be actions of violence, such as wrecking, damaging, beating, hitting, and killing. In fact, the seal form is of a hand holding a stick or club.

毀

毀 huǐ
Destroy, ruin, damage; defame, slander.

毅 yì
Firm, resolute.

毆（殴） ōu
Beat up, hit.

殺（杀） shā
Kill, slaughter; fight.

enclosure

There is no question as to the meaning of this radical, and its relationship to its characters. Anything with a boundary of some sort is included. For a country, this would be the territorial borders, a drawing usually has a frame, a garden will have its hedges, fences or walls, and a prison its four depressing grey walls!

困 kùn
Be stranded, be hard pressed; surround, pin down; tired; sleepy.

回 huí
Circle, winding; return, turn around; chapter.

圍(围) wéi
Enclose, surround; around.

圈 quān
Ring, ring-shaped
articles; sphere, scope,
circle; encircle, surround;
to mark with a circle.

固 gù
Solid, firm; resolutely;
consolidate; originally,
in the first place; no
doubt.

國（国） guó
Country, state, nation;
of the state, national.

園（园） yuán
Garden, area of land for
growing plants.

圓（圆） yuán
Round, circular,
spherical; tactful,
satisfactory; justify.

圖（图） tú
Picture, drawing; chart,
map; scheme, plan;
pursue, seek; intention.

團（团） tuán
Round, circular; shaped
like a ball; roll; invite;
group, society,
organization; regiment;
a measure word.

zhǐ

to stop

RADICAL 77

Under this particular radical, there are two completely opposed characters: 正 (straight, upright, pure), and 歪 (crooked, devious). The fascinating feature of 歪 is in its combination of the two characters 不 (not) and 正 (straight) – literally, crooked is not straight!

正

歧 qí
Fork, branch; divergent, different.

正 zhèng
Straight, upright; in the middle; punctual; honest, upright; pure; principal, chief; regular; positive; exactly.

步

此 cǐ
This place, here; this kind, such as these.

步 bù
Step, pace; step; condition; walk; tread.

歲(岁) suì
Year; àge.

武

歷(历) lì
Undergo, experience; one by one; calendar.

武 wǔ
Military; connected wtih boxing skill, swordplay, martial arts; chivalrous, valiant, fierce.

歪

歸(归) guī
Return, go back to, give back to; come together; turn over to.

歪 wāi
Crooked, slanting; devious, underhand.

shì

sign

RADICAL 113

ネ

The manifestation of this radical in a character at once indicates that its meaning will be based on something of a divine nature, or pertaining to the spiritual – whether this be benign or evil. Meditation and worship, blessings like good fortune (福) and status (祿) bear this radical. However, 鬼 couples with 祟 in an oft-heard idiom 鬼鬼祟祟 (stealthy, furtive).

禮

禍(祸) huò
Misfortune, disaster; bring disaster upon, ruin.

禮(礼) lǐ
Ceremony, rite; courtesy, manners, etiquette; gift, present.

祥 xiáng
Auspicious, propitious, lucky.

祈禱(祈祷) qídǎo
Pray, ask earnestly, entreat.

禪(禅) chán
Deep meditation.

祠 cí
Ancestral temple.

福 fú
Good fortune, blessing, happiness.

祿 lù
Salary, official pay.

社 shè
Organized body, society, agency.

祖 zǔ
Grandfather; ancestor; founder of a craft, religious sect, school of thought, etc.

祝 zhù
Express good wishes.

神 shén
Supernatural, magical; God, deity; spirit, mind; expression.

祟 suì
Evil spirit, ghost.

攴

knock

攵

RADICAL 66

The hand is engaged in the activity of knocking or hitting, or, as the case may be, rescuing (救), releasing (放), changing (改), receiving (收), scattering (散) and teaching (教). In the other characters, many denote actions of attacking, fighting, beating.

數

改 gǎi
Change, transfer; alter, revise; rectify; switch over to.

教 jiāo
Teach, instruct.

敵 (敌) dí
Enemy, foe; fight.

數 (数) shù
Number, figure.

放

放 fàng
Let go, release; let off; expand; blossom, open, put in, add to; put, place; send away; show.

政 zhèng
Politics; administrative aspects of government.

攻 gōng
Attack; accuse; study, specialize in.

散

救 jiù
Save; help.

敗(败) bài
Defeat, fail; counteract; decay, wither.

敢 gǎn
Bold, courageous; dare, have the confidence to.

敲

散 sǎn
Come loose, fall apart; scattered.

敬 jìng
Respect; offer politely and respectfully.

敲 qiāo
Knock, beat; fleece, overcharge.

勹

wrap

RADICAL 20

The action of wrapping also connotes embracing or enveloping of something. What is shown in the seal character appears to be a person bent over and with arms curved. The body is curved and bundled up in the state of creeping and crawling (匍匐). To gang up with (勾) has the 'wrap' or 'envelop' radical containing a hook.

包

匍匐　púfú
Crawl, creep; lie prostrate.

勾　gōu
Cancel, cross out; draw; induce, gang up with.

包　bāo
Wrap; bundle, package; protuberance; include, contain; guarantee; hire.

98

CHARACTERISTICS

辛　力
白　广
黑　幺
大　老
方　歹

辛

xīn

bitter

辛

RADICAL 160

In the main, the most common examples show the radical on both sides. For instance, 'manage' has 力 or 'strength' squeezed in the middle (辦); 'differentiate' has 刂 or a curved 'knife' in the centre (辨); 'argue' naturally has 言, 'speech' in its midst (辯); and 'braid' has the insertion of 糸, 'silk' (辮).

辭 (辞) cí
Diction; a type of classical Chinese literature; take leave; decline; dismiss; shirk.

辮 (辫) biàn
Plait, braid; pigtail.

100

辣 là
Spicy, peppery, hot; stinging (of smell or taste); vicious, ruthless.

辜 gū
Guilt, crime.

辟 bì
Monarch, sovereign; ward off, keep away.

辟 pì
Open up (territory, land), break (ground); penetrating, incisive; refute, repudiate.

辨(办) bàn
Do, manage, attend to; set up, prepare; punish (legally), administer justice.

辨 biàn
Differentiate, distinguish, discriminate.

辯(辩) biàn
Argue, dispute, debate.

bái

white

RADICAL 106

White is equivalent to purity. Therefore, the emperor or sovereign, traditionally regarded as invested with supreme authority, is expected to have an unblemished record. The character for 'emperor' is written with the 'white' radical.

皎 jiǎo
Clear and bright.

皓 hào
White; bright, luminous.

魄 pò
Soul; vigour, spirit.

皇 huáng
Emperor, sovereign.

hēi

black

RADICAL 203

Just as white stands for purity and brightness, black represents darkness, gloom and defilement, certainly less positive attributes. Bring together 'black' (黑) and 'out' (出), and the result is the character for dismissal (黜).

默　mò
Silent, tacit; write from memory.

黛　dài
A black pigment used by women in ancient times to paint their eyebrows.

黜　chù
Remove somebody from office, dismiss.

大 dà

big

RADICAL 37

A man with hands outstretched – which has evolved into the character for 'big'. In 'sky' or 'heaven', an additional horizontal stroke is added on top of the man, suggesting a higher authority. However, in a few of the characters where the 'big' radical is placed above, the meanings are those of mastery or power.

套

天 tiān
Sky; day; weather; nature; God; Heaven.

失 shī
Lose; miss; mistake; break (a promise).

套 tào
Sheath, cover; cover with; overlap; harness; knot; copy; formula.

奇 qí
Strange, rare, unusual;
surprise, wonder.

奔 bēn
Run quickly; hurry,
hasten, rush; flee.

奏 zòu
Play (music), perform
(on a musical
instrument); achieve,
produce.

奕 yì
Radiating power and
vitality.

奪(夺) duó
Take by force, seize;
compete, contend for;
deprive.

奘 zhuǎng
Big and thick, stout,
robust.

獎(奖) jiǎng
Encourage, praise,
reward.

奮(奋) fèn
Exert oneself, act
vigorously; raise, lift.

方 fāng

square

RADICAL 70

Also a derivative of 'man' (人) and 'big' (大), 方 is like a man whose shoulders are squared, hence the meaning. This is again, however, one of those radicals which do not actively contribute to meaning, which should be apparent from the examples listed.

旁

施 shī
Execute, carry out; bestow, grant; impose; apply.

旁 páng
Side; other, else.

旅

旌 jīng
Ancient banner.

旅 lǚ
Travel; brigade; troops.

旖旎 yǐnǐ
Charming and gentle.

族

族 zú
Clan; race or nationality; class or group.

於 yú
Towards, out of, up to.

旗 qí
Flag, banner.

旗

旋 xuán
Revolve, circle; return; soon.

lì

strength

RADICAL 19

Signs of industry and exertion mark the 'strength' radical. The character for 'move' attaches 'heavy' (重) on the left to the radical (力) on the right – applying energy to a heavy object. Similarly, 'encourage' (勉) and (勸) need strength, and definitely 'success' (勝) also derives from having put in strength and energy.

勁(劲) jìng
Strong, powerful, sturdy.

勇 yǒng
Brave, courageous.

勉 miǎn
Exert, strive; encourage.

動(动) dòng
Move; act; change; touch; arouse (emotion).

動

務(务) wù
Affair, business; be engaged in doing.

勝(胜) shèng
Victory, success; surpass; wonderful; be equal to.

勞(劳) láo
Work, labour; fatigue; meritorious deed, service.

勞

勢(势) shì
Power, force; circumstances, situation; sign, gesture.

勤 qín
Industrious, hardworking; frequently, regularly.

勸(劝) quàn
Advise, urge, persuade; encourage.

努 nǔ
Exert, put in (strength).

助

助 zhù
Help, assist, aid.

功 gōng
Merit, achievement; skill; work.

disease

RADICAL 104

At one glance, 疒 is a radical which unmistakably signifies disease. Starting from the blanket character for a sick condition (病), one soon finds that it forms the root of every imaginable affliction – insanity, emaciation, malaria (瘧), smallpox, paralysis (癱), cancer (癌), to name but a few.

病 bìng
Sick, ill; disease; fault, defect.

症 zhèng
Disease, illness.

癲(癫) diān
Mentally deranged; insane.

癢(痒) yǎng
Itchy, ticklish.

疼

疲　pǐ
Tired, weary, exhausted.

疼　téng
Ache, pain, sore; love
dearly, dote on.

痛　tòng
Ache, pain; sadness;
extremely.

瘤　liú
Tumour.

痕

痰　tán
Phlegm, sputum.

瘋（疯）fēng
Mad, insane, crazy.

痘　dòu
Smallpox.

痕　hén
Mark, trace; scar.

瘋

瘡（疮）chuāng
Sore, skin ulcer; wound.

痴　chī
Silly, idiotic; crazy
about; insane, mad.

瘦　shòu
Thin, emaciated;
infertile, poor.

疤　bā
Scar.

幺

yāo

slender

RADICAL 52

幺 , 'slender', manifests itself in a character like 幼, which pertains to youthfulness. Putting 幺 beside 力, strength, the meaning comes across as 'to possess small strength'. And in 幽, the radical appears twice nestled inside a frame, reinforcing the meaning of 'secret' or 'hidden'.

幼

幻 huàn
Imaginary, illusory; magical, changeable.

幼 yòu
Young, underage; children, the young.

幽 yōu
Deep and remote; secret, hidden; quiet; imprison; of the nether world.

lǎo

old

RADICAL 125

Although the contemporary meaning of 考 is 'to examine' or 'to investigate', in the past it also meant 'aged', 'longevity', 'ancestors'. The former meanings have become obsolete, but the character still bears the 'old' radical. 者 being an auxiliary noun, carries no intrinsic meaning.

考

考 kǎo
Give or take a test or quiz; check, inspect; investigate, verify.

者 zhě
Auxiliary noun – that which is, who is. Referring to a person.

歹

dǎi

bad

RADICAL 78

Because the character original-ly written on shell is in the shape of a skeleton and a broken fragment of bone, the notion of death and destruc-tion marks the majority of the examples. These include 殄 (exterminate), 殉 (sacrifice one's life), 殮 (put one's body into a coffin), 殃 (disaster).

殞

殘(残) cán
Incomplete, deficient; remnant; injure, damage; savage, cruel.

殞(殒) yǔn
Perish, die.

死 sǐ
Die; deadly; rigid, inflexible; impassable.

NUMERALS

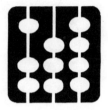

yī

one

RADICAL 1

Radicals under categories of Numerals and Basic Strokes do not provide a meaning to the characters listed under them. What has happened is that those characters which do not come under any other radical are classified here. For example, 上 and 下, 世, 丁, all share the horizontal stroke, and are put willy-nilly under the 'one' radical.

丁 dīng
Man; family members, population; the fourth of the ten Heavenly Stems; fourth.

且 qiě
Just; for a long time; even; both.

116

上 shàng
Up; higher, superior;
first (part); go up; go
to; enter; apply.

下 xià
Below, under, down;
lower, inferior; next,
second; descend; take
away.

世 shì
Life, lifetime; age,
era; generation;
world.

丙 bǐng
The third of the ten
Heavenly Stems; third.

丑 chǒu
The second of the
twelve Earthly
Branches; clown.

丢 diū
Lose; throw; put aside.

bā

eight

RADICAL 12

Eight also performs as a radical because several characters possessing two downward strokes resemble the character for 'eight'. These two strokes are often found at the bottom, but as in 公 it is also written on top.

其 qí
His, her, its, their; that, such.

具 jù
Utensil, tool; possess, have; provide; a measure word.

字典

典　diǎn
Standard, law; literary quotation; ceremony; mortgage.

兼　jiān
Double; twice; simultaneously.

冀　jì
Hope, long for.

公共

男　女

公　gōng
Public; common, general; impartial; official business; male.

共　gòng
Common, general; share; together; altogether.

兮　xī
A gale has risen and is sweeping in clouds across the sky.

兵

兵　bīng
Weapons, arms; soldier; army, troops; military.

六　liù
Six.

shí

ten

RADICAL 24

The general 十 shape present in this group of characters justifies their belonging to this radical. In the case of 博 and 協, the horizontal stroke is shrunk, and forms the left part of the character.

升

升 shēng
Rise, ascend; promote.

午 wǔ
Noon, midday; the seventh of the twelve Earthly Branches.

卑

卑 bēi
Low; inferior; modest.

半 bàn
Half; in the middle;
very little; partly.

卉 huì
Various kinds of grass.

千 qiān
Thousand; a great
number of.

博

協(协) xié
Joint, common; assist.

南 nán
South.

博 bó
Rich, abundant; win,
gain.

卓

卅 sà
Thirty.

卓 zhuō
Tall and erect; eminent,
distinguished, outstan-
ding.

èr

two

RADICAL 7

The two horizontal strokes are incorporated in the character 井, whilst in others like 亞 and 互, they form the two horizontal boundaries. 五 is also classified under the 'two' radical.

井

互 hù
Mutual, each other.

井 jǐng
Well; pit, mine; neat, orderly.

亞(亚) yà
Inferior; second.

BASIC STROKES

RADICAL 4

A stroke slanting downwards to the left, this radical has belonging to it such a variety of characters like 久 and 乘 . The downward stroke, however, does not always appear at the same angle.

乘

久 jiǔ
For a long time; how long?

乖 guāi
Well-behaved, good; clever, alert.

乘 chéng
Ride; take advantage of; multiply.

儿

乙 yǐ

乚

乙 in its variant form is a downward stroke with a little hook at the end. It offers no distinct meaning, although the ancient shell form is of a meandering river.

亂

乙 yǐ
The second of the ten Heavenly Stems; second.

亂(乱) luàn
In disorder; chaos, turmoil; confused; random.

乾(干) gān
Dry; empty.

儿

APPENDIX

Pinyin	Simplified	Regular	Meaning
zhēng		掙	struggle
zhēng		猙	ferocious
zhēng		崢	steep
zhēng	（铮）	錚	metallic clang
zhēng		箏	string instrument
tōng		通	passable
tǒng		桶	bucket
tǒng		捅	poke
tòng		痛	pain
tān	（摊）	攤	spread
tān	（滩）	灘	beach
tān	（瘫）	癱	paralyse
lí		狸	fox
lí		厘	unit of measure
lǐ		俚	rude
lǐ		理	structure
lǐ	（鲤）	鯉	carp
mái		埋	bury

Pinyin	Simplified	Regular	Meaning
tāi		胎	embryo
tái		抬	lift
tái		苔	moss
tái	（台）	颱	typhoon
shǐ		始	beginning
huǐ		悔	regret
huì		晦	dark
huì	（诲）	誨	teach
hǎi		海	sea
méi		梅	plum
méi		酶	yeast
qiàn		歉	bad harvest
qiàn		慊	hateful
xián		嫌	suspicion
fān		幡	streamers
fān		翻	turn over
fán		蕃	luxuriant
fán		璠	a jade
fán		燔	roast
fán		蹯	paws
pán		蟠	coil

Pinyin	Simplified	Regular	Meaning
kū		枯	withered
kū		骷	skeleton
kǔ		苦	bitter
gū		估	estimate
gū		咕	coo
gū		沽	buy and sell
gū		姑	aunt
gū		酤	wine
gū		辜	crime
gū	（诂）	詁	layman terms
gǔ		牯	cow
gù		固	firm
gù		痼	bad habit

tī		梯	ladder
tì		剃	shave
tì		涕	mucus
dì		睇	look askance
dì		第	position

mēng	（蒙）	矇	deceive
méng		獴	mongoose
méng		檬	lemon
méng		朦	misty

Pinyin	Simplified	Regular	Meaning
láo	（劳）	勞	labour
láo	（唠）	嘮	nag
láo	（痨）	癆	tuberculosis
lāo	（捞）	撈	dredge
láng		狼	wolf
láng		琅	a jade
láng		郎	gentleman
láng		廊	verandah
lǎng		朗	bright
làng		浪	waves
gěng		哽	choke
gěng	（绠）	綆	rope attached to a bucket
gěng		梗	stem
gěng	（鲠）	鯁	fish-bone
dīng	（钉）	釘	nail
dīng		盯	watch closely
dīng		叮	inquire into
dìng	（订）	訂	arrange
qiáo		憔	haggard
qiáo		樵	firewood
qiáo		瞧	look

Pinyin	Simplified	Regular	Meaning
fén	（坟）	坟	grave
fén	（濆）	濆	highland alongside a river
fèn	（偾）	僨	ruin
fèn	（愤）	憤	anger
jùn		俊	handsome
jùn		峻	steep
jùn	（骏）	駿	noble steed
jùn		竣	finish
suō		唆	instigate
suō		梭	weaving shuttle
quān		悛	repent
ráng		瓤	pulp
rǎng		壤	soil
rǎng		攘	reject
rǎng		嚷	yell
ràng	（让）	讓	make way
shēn		伸	stretch
shēn		呻	groan
shēn	（绅）	紳	gentry
shēn		砷	arsenic
shén		神	God

Pinyin	Simplified	Regular	Meaning
tiāo		佻	frivolous
tiāo		挑	choose
tiào		眺	gaze
tiào		跳	jump
tiǎo		窕	refined
yáo	（谣）	謠	ballad
yáo	（徭）	徭	forced labour
yáo	（摇）	搖	shake
yáo	（瑶）	瑤	beautiful jade
zǎo		澡	bathe
zào		噪	make noise
zào		燥	dry
zào		躁	impatient
zhōng	（钟）	鍾	goblet
zhǒng	（肿）	腫	swollen
zhòng	（种）	種	grow
zhǒng		踵	heal
xiáng	（详）	詳	thorough
yáng		佯	pretend
yáng		洋	ocean
yǎng		氧	oxygen

Pinyin	Simplified	Regular	Meaning
zhū	（朱）	硃	scarlet
zhū		侏	dwarf
zhū	（诛）	誅	execute
zhū		珠	pearl
zhū		株	exposed roots of a tree
zhū		蛛	spider
zhù		住	stay
zhù		注	notice
zhù	（驻）	駐	be stationed
zhù		柱	pillar
zhù		蛀	decay
zū		租	rent
zǔ	（诅）	詛	curse
zǔ		阻	obstruct
zǔ	（组）	組	organize
zǔ		祖	ancestors
jǔ		沮	stop
jǔ		咀	chew
jiě		姐	sister
cū		粗	rough
kǎo		拷	flog
kǎo		烤	roast
kào	（铐）	銬	handcuff

Pinyin	Simplified	Regular	Meaning
dú	（独）	獨	solitary
zhú	（烛）	燭	candle
chù	（触）	觸	touch
zhuó	（浊）	濁	muddy
zhuó	（镯）	鐲	bracelet
zhāo		招	beckon
shào		劭	exhort
shào	（绍）	紹	continue
zhāo		昭	obvious
zhǎo		沼	pond
zhào	（诏）	詔	instruct
diāo		貂	sable
pǐ		劈	split
pǐ		癖	addiction
pì		僻	secluded
pì		譬	analogy
pī		霹	thunderbolt
kǎn		砍	chop
chuī		吹	blow
kǎn		坎	ridge
yǐn	（饮）	飲	drink
chuī		炊	cook

Pinyin	Simplified	Regular	Meaning
tuó	（驼）	駝	camel
tuó	（鸵）	鴕	ostrich
tuó		陀	a top
duò		舵	rudder
hè		褐	coarse cloth
hè		喝	drink
kě		渴	thirsty
gé		葛	creeping plant
mù		募	solicit
mù		墓	tomb
mù		幕	tent
mù		暮	dusk
mù		慕	admire
méi		媒	matchmaker
méi		煤	coal
móu	（谋）	謀	strategy
tíng		蜓	dragonfly
tíng		霆	thunderclap
tíng		庭	courtyard
tǐng		挺	stick up
tǐng		艇	small boat

Pinyin	Simplified	Regular	Meaning
jiǎ		假	false
xiá		瑕	red stain on a jade
xiá		暇	leisure
xiá		霞	rosy clouds
xiá		遐	distant
xiā	（虾）	蝦	prawn

Pinyin	Simplified	Regular	Meaning
zhān		沾	moisten
zhàn		站	stand
zhān		粘	paste
tie	（贴）	貼	allowance
tiē		帖	invitation

Pinyin	Simplified	Regular	Meaning
tóng		桐	tung tree
tóng	（铜）	銅	bronze
tóng		筒	tube-shaped container
dòng		峒	cave
dòng		恫	threaten
dòng		洞	hole
dòng		胴	large intestines

骷 苦 枯 酤 姑